THE WORLD ALMANAC & ⬡ MENSA

BRAIN GAMES
WORLD TOUR

101 ✈
MIND-SHARPENING
PUZZLES

DAVID MILLAR

WORLD ALMANAC BOOKS

World Almanac books may be purchased in bulk at special discounts for sales promotion, corporate gifts, fund-raising, or educational purposes. Special editions can also be created to specifications. For details, contact the Special Sales Department, 307 West 36th Street, 11th Floor, New York, NY 10018 or info@skyhorsepublishing.com.

Published by World Almanac Books, an imprint of Skyhorse Publishing, Inc., 307 West 36th Street, 11th Floor, New York, NY 10018.

The World Almanac® is a registered trademark of Skyhorse Publishing, Inc. All rights reserved.

www.skyhorsepublishing.com

10 9 8 7 6 5 4 3 2 1

Puzzles and text by David Millar
Interior design by Chris Schultz
Cover design by Kai Texel

Library of Congress Cataloging-in-Publication Data is available on file.

ISBN: 978-1-5107-7605-0

Printed in the United States of America

Contents

Acknowledgments

This book is dedicated to Jim Bumgardner, who made my first trip to the West Coast possible, and Thomas Ciszek, whose photos of Santa Monica sunsets inspire me to return as often as possible.

Thanks to my test-solvers:

- Ashley Goverman
- Jeffrey Bardon
- Martin Ender
- Christian König
- Psyho
- Prasanna Seshadri
- Marco Wahnschafft
- Additional anonymous puzzlers of Discord

... and thank you for solving!

David Millar

Puzzles

Skyscrapers & Alleys 1

Place a skyscraper in each square, with a height from 1 to 6, so that no two buildings in the same row or column have the same number of floors. Each number outside of the grid represents the number of buildings visible when looking into the grid from the clue. Taller buildings block shorter buildings from view. Each number inside an alley represents the total number of buildings visible looking outward from its position.

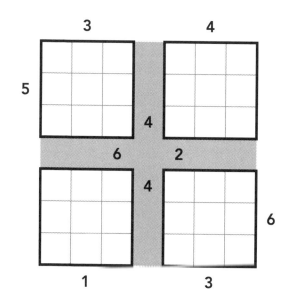

Numcross 1

Use the provided clues to fill the grid with numbers. No entry may start with a 0.

A	B	C		D	E	F
G				H		
I		▮	J		▮	▮
▮	K	L			M	▮
▮	▮	N		▮	O	P
Q	R		▮	S		
T			▮	U		

Across

A. A perfect square
D. O across × S down
G. P down × 3
H. Q across – 10
I. Another perfect square
J. Another perfect square
K. Contains one of every odd digit
N. Another perfect square
O. C down + 1
Q. E down × F down
S. O across × C down
T. K across / N across
U. N across × C down

Down

A. J down – 1
B. Digits that sum to S down
C. Sum of the digits in Q across and S across
D. Digits that sum to F down
E. T across / N across
F. One-fifth of P down
J. R down × 5
L. Digits that sum to J across
M. A palindrome
P. Another perfect square
Q. One-half of A down
R. A perfect cube
S. O across + 1

Country Road 1

Draw a single, continuous, nonintersecting loop moving through the grid and visiting each boldly-outlined region exactly once. A region displaying a number indicates the number of cells visited in that region. Non-visited cells from two different regions mustn't share an edge.

6			2			2	2	4			
									3		
							3				1
	8				2	3		4			
1	3		3		3		7				
	4										
4						6					
		2		2			2				
3											

Story Logic 1

A great way to get to know another city is to check out a local food truck park. Use the clues to match the names of the trucks with the assigned spaces where they'll be set up, their side dishes, and what time they'll be up on the band's stage raffling off a gift certificate.

	Space A	Space B	Space C	Space D	Space E	Space F	Bacon Green Beans	Green Chile Corn	Potato Salad	Seasoned Fries	Tex-Mex Corn	Truffle Mac	3:30 PM	4:15 PM	5:00 PM	5:45 PM	6:30 PM	7:15 PM
Crepe Fusion																		
Quill and Quark																		
Smokin' Hawg Q																		
Tacos Lo Quiero																		
Taqueria Ana Luisa																		
Terry's BBQ																		
3:30 PM																		
4:15 PM																		
5:00 PM																		
5:45 PM																		
6:30 PM																		
7:15 PM																		
Bacon Green Beans																		
Green Chile Corn																		
Potato Salad																		
Seasoned Fries																		
Tex-Mex Corn																		
Truffle Mac																		

1. The taquerias both have spaces located closest to the parking lot.

2. The latest raffles will be from the trucks closest to the stage.

3. Crepe Fusion is located between the two trucks serving corn side dishes, all on the same side of the park.

4. Quill and Quark is holding their raffle 45 minutes after Taqueria Ana Luisa, and 45 minutes before Terry's BBQ.

5. Tacos Lo Quiero will hold their raffle 45 minutes after the truck serving Seasoned Fries.

6. Crepe Fusion is located directly across the park from the truck holding the 3:30 PM raffle.

7. Taqueria Ana Luisa, which is serving the Potato Salad, will hold their raffle sometime after Smokin' Hawg Q's raffle.

8. The Green Chile Corn is being served by one of the first three trucks holding a raffle.

9. Smokin' Hawg Q serves the Bacon Green Beans.

10. Truffle Mac is being served at space D, which is not Terry's BBQ truck.

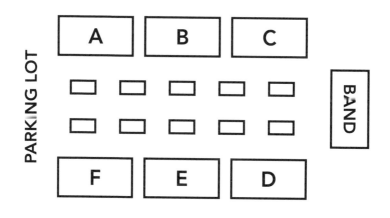

Scenic Route 1

Use the clues to determine pairs of words that fit the blanks provided. Each pair will feature one shorter word with only some of the letters, and one longer word that features all of the letters. When complete, the numbered blanks will spell the name of a travel destination.

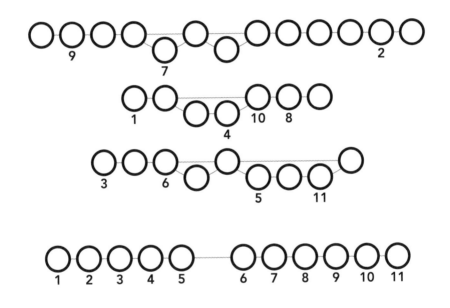

Faster Routes	Scenic Routes
By design	Big-mouthed water bird
Mention	Catch-up/update course
Variety of tree nut	Spanning several countries

Rearrangement 1-2

Rearrange the letters in A PANORAMIC INSET to spell the name of a West Coast attraction too long to capture with a non-panoramic photo.

Rearrange the letters in GULLS IN FORECASTS to spell a place you might hang out while waiting to fly to a tropical destination.

Transit Map 1

Use the clues to fill the bus route with letters to form words both northbound and southbound.

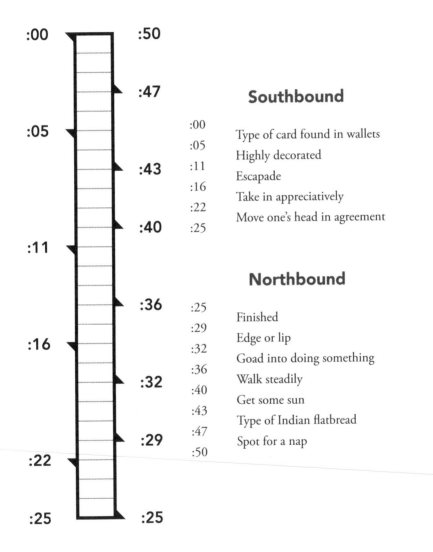

Southbound

:00
:05   Type of card found in wallets
:11   Highly decorated
:16   Escapade
:22   Take in appreciatively
:25   Move one's head in agreement

Northbound

:25
:29   Finished
:32   Edge or lip
:36   Goad into doing something
:40   Walk steadily
:43   Get some sun
:47   Type of Indian flatbread
:50   Spot for a nap

Rows Garden 1

Using the clues provided, enter a letter into each triangle to fill the garden. Each row contains one or two entries, and each hexagonal flower contains a six-letter word wrapped around the center. It's up to you to determine where to place the starting letter and the direction of the word.

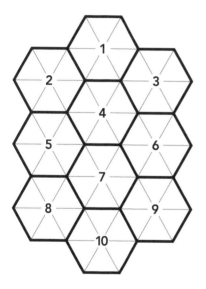

Everything

Celebrity / Decorate with crayons

Whip / Measuring tool

Zoo item / Garden Occupant

SNL alum Fey / Simple beverage

Rice flour dessert / Imperial unit

Some devotees / Road edge

Vehicle

Flowers

1. Pet wearable
2. Parade features
3. Gas station grill type
4. Metal-adjacent genre
5. Hollywood profession

6, Out there
7. Island state
8. By no means unique
9. Late-morning meal
10. Signs of breakage

Numcross 2

Use the provided clues to fill the grid with numbers. No entry may start with a 0.

A	B	C			D	E
F			G		H	
I		■	J	K		
■		L			■	■
M	N			■	O	P
Q		■	R	S		
T		■		U		

Across

A. M down × 2

D. Sum of the digits in B down

F. Digits that sum to L down

H. L down − 5

I. One-seventh of S down

J. A down × C down + 1000

L. D across × K down

M. R across − 800

O. S down − 4

Q. A perfect cube

R. D across × E down

T. Another perfect cube

U. A multiple of D across

Down

A. A across − 1

B. Odd digits that sum to D across

C. A perfect square

D. A multiple of I across

E. N down + 1

G. Contains one of every odd digit

K. I across + 8

L. D across × 2

M. K down × 6

N. O across × 2

O. Digits sum to H across

P. M down × 6

S. Q across + T across

Cube Logic 1

Which of the two templates can be folded to produce the exact same crate?

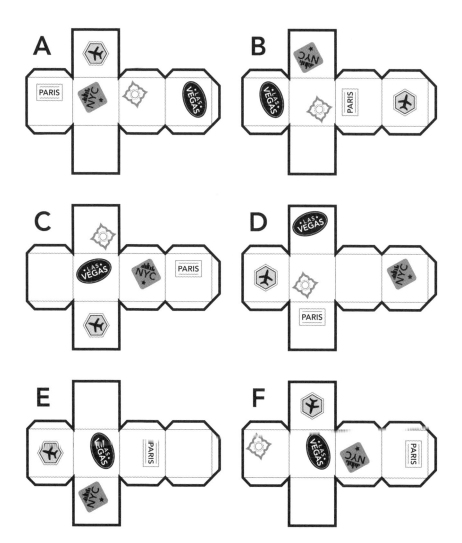

Rebus Travel Agency 1

This travel agency has some unusual ways of advertising travel destinations. Can you figure out where they want to send travelers?

Symbol Sums 1

The sums of five combinations of symbols have been provided. What is the value of each individual symbol?

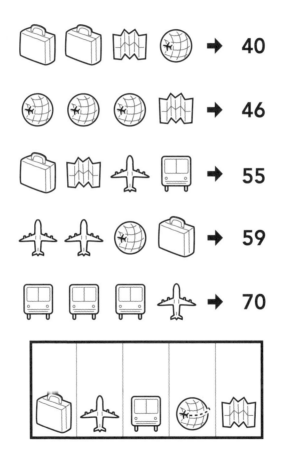

Throwing Shade 1

Shade some cells so the remaining letters in each row and column spell answers to the provided clues. Clues are sorted alphabetically by answer.

C	P	E	O	S	V	C	E	R
C	R	V	S	E	E	P	V	O
L	O	R	E	Y	P	O	A	L
O	I	T	H	N	E	R	S	C
C	O	V	I	A	E	R	N	L
S	A	E	O	T	G	A	S	H
E	S	R	W	C	A	P	C	O
E	T	R	A	E	A	T	C	L
M	T	M	O	H	N	T	H	L

Rows

- Obscure
- Key on a keyboard (abbr.)
- Having integrity
- Vinaigrette component
- Time period
- "None of the above"
- Take back (abbr.)
- Video game company
- Snack

Columns

- Shut
- Per item
- Facial feature
- Midwestern state
- Actor Chris
- Baked good
- Bird dwelling
- Word or phrase
- Animal non-consumer

Word Sudoku 1

Place one of each letter from BALTIMORE into each row, column, and 3 × 3 box without repetition.

				T	O		I	L
B						E		
	A				L			
		L	T				A	M
E				I				R
A	I			M	O			
			E				R	
		I						E
O	B		R	A				

Rearrangement 3-4

Rearrange the letters in BOUNCERS FELT ONSET to spell something a couple of clubgoers might need if they trade a night at the club for a day at the beach.

Rearrange the letters in FED BABE TANKARDS to spell a place where a couple might wake up and have a leisurely morning meal.

Rows Garden 2

Using the clues provided, enter a letter into each triangle to fill the garden. Each row contains one or two entries, and each hexagonal flower contains a six-letter word wrapped around the center. It's up to you to determine where to place the starting letter and the direction of the word.

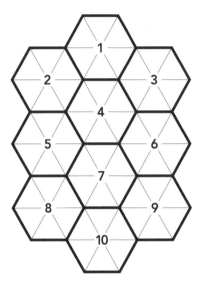

Spouse's female parent, inf.

Rice dish / Football field unit

Laser print material / Coffee holders

After dark / Unused

Famed chair designer / 12:00 PM

Something won / Crafty online market

One's formal education

Popular talk series

Flowers

1. Relatives

2. Tea brand

3. Security staff

4. Off-grid loner

5. Mystery

6. Pasta unit

7. Allergy season result

8. Cricket noises

9. Greedy

10. Pillaged

Numcross 3

Use the provided clues to fill the grid with numbers. No entry may start with a 0.

A	B			C	D	
E			F			
G		H				
I				J	K	L
		M	N			
	O				P	
	Q				R	

Across

A. A perfect cube

C. O down − 2

E. A perfect square

F. A multiple of R across

G. A "full house"

I. A across × 6

J. A palindrome

M. A multiple of P across whose digits sum to R across

O. Another perfect square

P. Sum of the digits in B down

Q. E across + 1

R. A number between O down and P across

Down

A. Digits that sum to O down

B. Consecutive digits not in order

C. One-fifth of H down

D. One-half of N down

F. O down + P across

H. Contains one of every even digit

K. One-fourth of C down

L. Year of Kubrick's "Space Odyssey"

N. Another perfect cube

O. One-half of P across

Skyscrapers & Alleys 2

Place a skyscraper in each square, with a height from 1 to 6, so that no two buildings in the same row or column have the same number of floors. Each number outside of the grid represents the number of buildings visible when looking into the grid from the clue. Taller buildings block shorter buildings from view. Each number inside an alley represents the total number of buildings visible looking outward from its position.

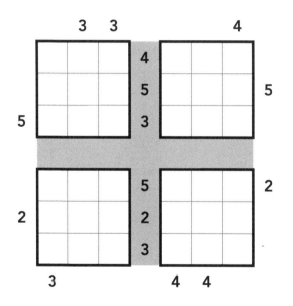

Country Road 2

Draw a single, continuous, nonintersecting loop moving through the grid and visiting each boldly-outlined region exactly once. A region displaying a number indicates the number of cells visited in that region. Non-visited cells from two different regions mustn't share an edge.

Rows Garden 3

Using the clues provided, enter a letter into each triangle to fill the garden. Each row contains one or two entries, and each hexagonal flower contains a six-letter word wrapped around the center. It's up to you to determine where to place the starting letter and the direction of the word.

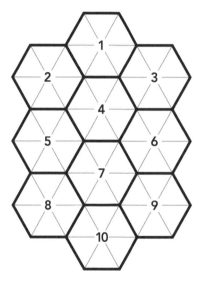

Create a sum

Ski location / Shopper's directives

Cut roughly / Cat distractor

Fat-centric diet / Display

Tall-growing grain / Prepared for defense

Elevated area / Ugly beast

Razor feature / Make music vocally

Consumed

Flowers

1.	Boat tool like an oar	**6.** Insist
2.	Place of education	**7.** Citrus fruit
3.	Fight against	**8.** For a gal about to wed
4.	Related to mail	**9.** Aromatic root
5.	Method of propulsion	**10.** Pacify

Story Logic 2

It's a busy day of shuttle runs between a local boutique hotel and several of the local airport's terminals. Use the clues to match the traveler to be picked up, the time of their flight, and their destination.

	10:15 AM	11:45 AM	1:30 PM	3:00 PM	Pasadena	Reno	San Diego	Tulsa
Glen								
Hilda								
Ike								
Jorge								
Pasadena								
Reno								
San Diego								
Tulsa								

1. Glen, whose flight does not depart earliest, is not going to Tulsa.

2. The flight to Reno is after Jorge's flight.

3. Hilda and Ike both have flights departing in the afternoon.

4. The flight to Pasadena departs 90 minutes after the flight to Reno.

5. Hilda is not going to Reno.

Cube Logic 2

Which of the two templates can be folded to produce the exact same crate?

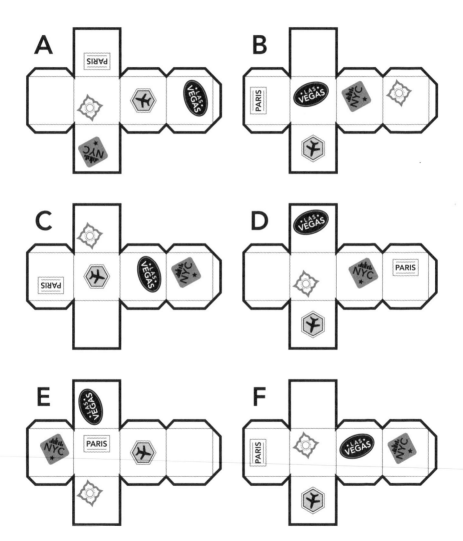

Rearrangement 5-6

Rearrange the letters in LIBYA FOREVER to spell a reason why travelers might spend time in an unexpected place.

Rearrange the letters in TIRED IRE OCCURS to spell a profession dedicated to keeping travelers from getting bored.

Throwing Shade 2

Shade some cells so the remaining letters in each row and column spell answers to the provided clues. Clues are sorted alphabetically by answer.

D	B	C	O	A	O	A	A	L
P	E	R	T	O	A	Y	W	L
U	O	R	O	A	F	E	T	E
L	E	A	F	P	A	S	T	A
O	I	U	L	S	L	E	O	D
P	N	A	S	T	A	S	T	A
P	G	N	A	W	T	S	E	D
C	G	E	S	R	T	I	T	S
K	S	O	T	E	C	K	M	S

Rows

- Consumed
- Christmas gift
- Obtain
- Chewed
- Part of a plant
- Cooking fat
- Starchy carb
- Attempt to infiltrate
- Different part of a plant

Columns

- Sense of amazement
- Some congressional votes
- Common paper bird
- Breakfast staple
- Uncarbonated
- Front
- Bit of grain
- Onomatopoeia example
- Symbolic item

Symbol Sums 2

The sums of five combinations of symbols have been provided. What is the value of each individual symbol?

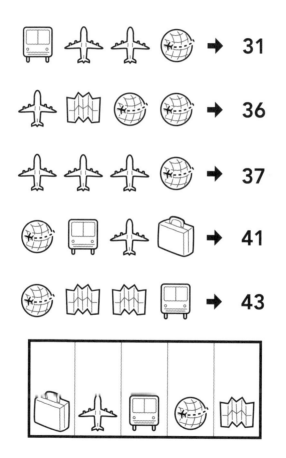

Transit Map 2

Use the clues to fill the bus route with letters to form words both northbound and southbound.

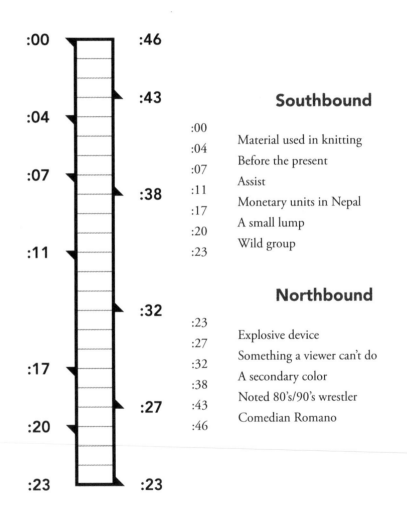

Southbound

:00
:04   Material used in knitting
:07   Before the present
:11   Assist
:17   Monetary units in Nepal
:20   A small lump
:23   Wild group

Northbound

:23
:27   Explosive device
:32   Something a viewer can't do
:38   A secondary color
:43   Noted 80's/90's wrestler
:46   Comedian Romano

Scenic Route 2

Use the clues to determine pairs of words that fit the blanks provided. Each pair will feature one shorter word with only some of the letters, and one longer word that features all of the letters. When complete, the numbered blanks will spell the name of a travel destination.

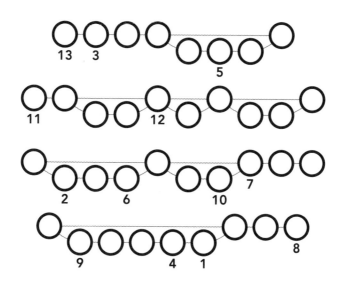

Faster Routes

Ill will

Journal

No longer fresh

Type of meat

Scenic Routes

Book of words

Made of many different pieces

Make more efficient

Stinging desert creature

Numcross 4

Use the provided clues to fill the grid with numbers. No entry may start with a 0.

A	B				C	D
E		F	G		H	
		I		J		
	K			L		
	M		N			
O			P		Q	R
S					T	

Across

A. I across – P across

C. Q down in reverse

E. Even digits that sum to L across

H. O down + R down

I. Year that Adam West's *Batman* debuted

K. One-half L across

L. Sum of the digits in M across

M. F down × 3

O. K across × 5

P. One-fourth of C down

S. O across – 20

T. R down × 5

Down

A. A across + 1

B. O across – 2

C. Some digits in descending order

D. A perfect square

F. Has two even digits and two odd digits

G. S across + D down

J. Digits that sum to A down

K. S across squared

N. D down + K across

O. Another perfect square

Q. D down – 2

R. Sum of the digits in P across

Rebus Travel Agency 2

This travel agency has some unusual ways of advertising travel destinations. Can you figure out where they want to send travelers?

Word Sudoku 2

Place one of each letter from SAN PIEDRO into each row, column, and 3 × 3 box without repetition.

		R		A		S		P
I			S		N		D	
						N		R
S	A	N						
			P	I	E			
						D	R	O
O		P						
	E		R		D			N
D		I		N		E		

Throwing Shade 3

Shade some cells so the remaining letters in each row and column spell answers to the provided clues. Clues are sorted alphabetically by answer.

S	W	W	A	M	L	M	P	P
E	L	R	W	M	A	A	C	O
M	A	E	U	R	S	H	H	A
O	S	C	P	A	K	I	I	S
I	T	D	L	O	A	L	K	D
A	S	R	O	W	A	M	P	T
L	T	O	A	W	E	E	L	D
T	E	P	D	L	I	M	D	L
E	E	K	L	E	M	L	M	E

Rows

- Tree
- Worshipped entity
- Wetland
- Decay
- Sport items
- Also wetland
- Lukewarm
- Dryer
- Home of Dr Pepper museum

Columns

- Missing, inf.
- Minor
- Unit of water
- A traditional gender
- Put online
- Make a boat go
- Go over briefly
- Destroy
- Garbage

Story Logic 3

It isn't easy keeping tabs on the character actors employed at the seventh greatest theme park in America. Use the clues to match each actor with the costume and the location they're assigned.

	Bumper Cars	Chip Shop	Drop Tower	Exit	Frog	Gopher	Horse	Iguana
Becky								
Celia								
Dennis								
Enrique								
Frog								
Gopher								
Horse								
Iguana								

1. Nobody's assigned location has the same first letter as their name.

2. Enrique was not assigned to a location with a ride.

3. Celia, who wore the frog costume, was not assigned to bumper cars.

4. Likewise, the staffer in the gopher costume was not assigned to the bumper cars.

5. Becky either had the horse costume or was set to work near the drop tower, but not both.

6. The chip shop is not where the staffer in the iguana costume was assigned.

7. The gopher-costumed employee was assigned either the chip shop or the exit.

8. Becky's costume was not the iguana.

Skyscrapers & Alleys 3

Place a skyscraper in each square, with a height from 1 to 6, so that
no two buildings in the same row or column have the same number
of floors. Each number outside of the grid represents the number
of buildings visible when looking into the grid from the clue. Taller
buildings block shorter buildings from view. Each number inside an
alley represents the total number of buildings visible looking outward
from its position.

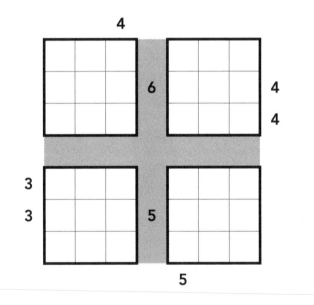

Transit Map 3

Use the clues to fill the bus route with letters to form words both northbound and southbound.

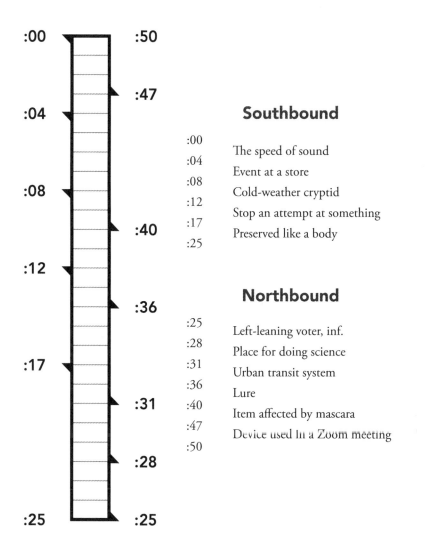

Southbound

:00
:04
:08
:12
:17
:25

The speed of sound
Event at a store
Cold-weather cryptid
Stop an attempt at something
Preserved like a body

Northbound

:25
:28
:31
:36
:40
:47
:50

Left-leaning voter, inf.
Place for doing science
Urban transit system
Lure
Item affected by mascara
Device used in a Zoom meeting

Country Road 3

Draw a single, continuous, nonintersecting loop moving through the grid and visiting each boldly-outlined region exactly once. A region displaying a number indicates the number of cells visited in that region. Non-visited cells from two different regions mustn't share an edge.

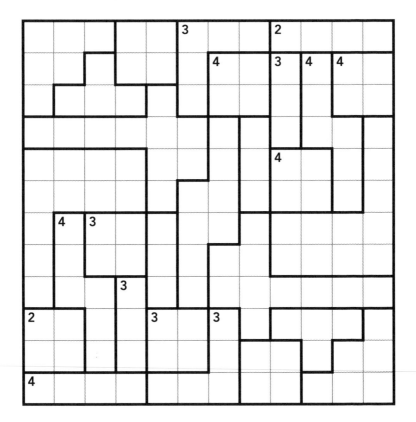

Cube Logic 3

Which of the two templates can be folded to produce the exact same crate?

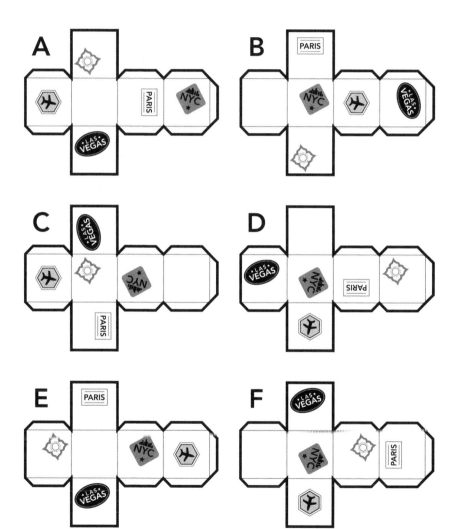

Scenic Route 3

Use the clues to determine pairs of words that fit the blanks provided.
Each pair will feature one shorter word with only some of the letters,
and one longer word that features all of the letters. When complete,
the numbered blanks will spell the name of a travel destination.

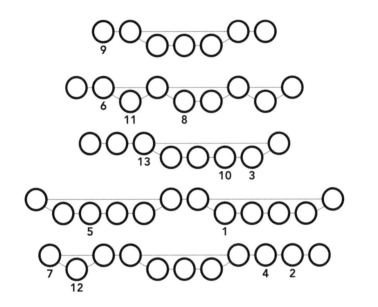

Faster Routes

A specific amphibian

Dangerous or risky

Not religious or spiritual

Put underground

Word or phrase

Scenic Routes

Breathtaking

Flavored like popcorn

Making a displeased look

Something found

Tumultuous weather

Rows Garden 4

Using the clues provided, enter a letter into each triangle to fill the garden. Each row contains one or two entries, and each hexagonal flower contains a six-letter word wrapped around the center. It's up to you to determine where to place the starting letter and the direction of the word.

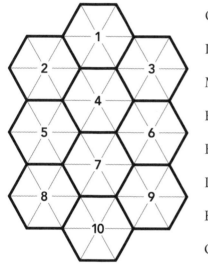

One's sense of self

Path / Matured

Mix / "Over the hill"

End of a river / Like some drinks

Even / Swap

Language symbol / Electricity, for example

East Asian country / Nonkosher meat type

Give a shot

Flowers

1. Hockey or soccer position
2. Attributes
3. Scour a body of water
4. Clothing modifier
5. Didn't pass

6. Span of ten years
7. Summary document
8. A certain sea creature
9. Do over
10. Kitchen storage

Rebus Travel Agency 3

This travel agency has some unusual ways of advertising travel destinations. Can you figure out where they want to send travelers?

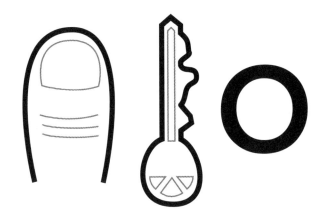

Rearrangement 7-8

Rearrange the letters in SUSTAIN VENDORS to spell some small businesses that cater specifically to tourists.

Rearrange the letters in NO GALLANT REDO to spell something for which you're unlikely to be refunded if you flip it over.

Cube Logic 4

Which of the four foldable patterns can be folded to make the crate displayed?

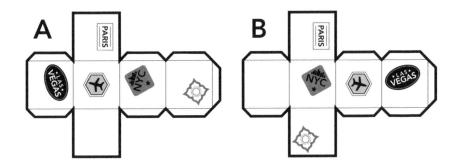

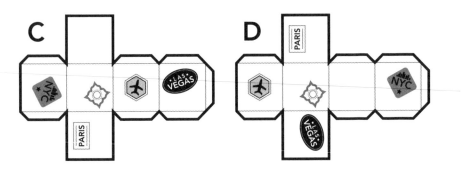

Symbol Sums 3

The sums of five combinations of symbols have been provided. What is the value of each individual symbol?

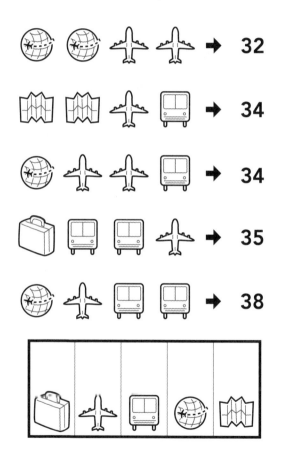

Numcross 5

Use the provided clues to fill the grid with numbers. No entry may start with a 0.

A	B	C	■	■	D	E
F			G	■	H	
■		I		J		
K	L		■	M		
N			O		■	■
P		■	Q		R	S
T		■	■	U		

Across

A. Digits that sum to R down

D. Sum of the digits in L down

F. Two pairs that sum to D across

H. One-fourth of U across

I. Contains one of each odd digit

K. Two digits followed by their sum in ascending order

M. Digits that sum to D across

N. A "full house"

P. A perfect square

Q. A palindrome

T. G down in reverse

U. R down + S down

Down

A. Another perfect square

B. A down – 30

C. L down × 6

D. Digits that sum to D across

E. One-fifth of I across

G. S down – P across

J. The digits of C down in descending order

K. L down – B down

L. E down + S down

O. S down in reverse

R. T across – H across

S. A multiple of 7

Throwing Shade 4

Shade some cells so the remaining letters in each row and column spell answers to the provided clues. Clues are sorted alphabetically by answer.

M	S	B	O	D	O	F	F	T
O	P	A	T	I	R	T	I	O
I	C	E	S	W	A	E	A	R
A	R	C	D	J	U	S	I	T
S	L	T	O	A	I	S	T	R
L	A	S	I	R	H	E	L	L
T	Y	O	L	D	K	E	C	K
E	R	E	L	D	I	T	A	X
N	P	R	R	T	E	S	T	T

Rows

- Curved segment
- Change
- Hideout
- Outdoor leisure space
- Take it easy
- Pillowy
- Curse
- Heat
- Egg part

Columns

- Someone in a movie
- Type of alcohol
- Worthless
- Sooner state citizen, inf.
- Earth
- Get wet
- Schoolwork
- Legal document
- Hospital section

Cube Logic 5

Which of the four foldable patterns can be folded to make the crate displayed?

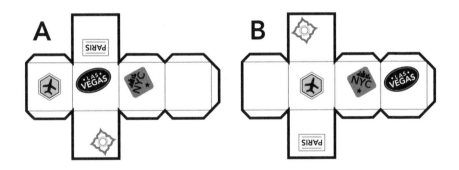

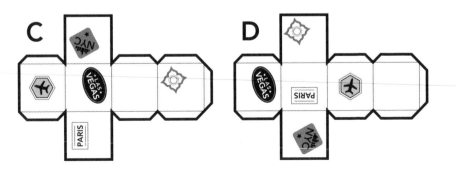

Transit Map 4

Use the clues to fill the bus route with letters to form words both northbound and southbound.

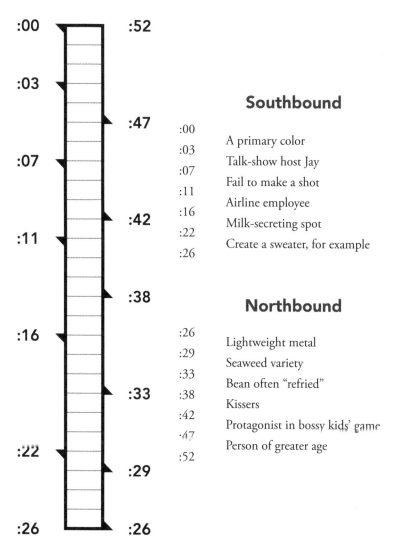

Southbound

:00
:03
:07
:11
:16
:22
:26

A primary color
Talk-show host Jay
Fail to make a shot
Airline employee
Milk-secreting spot
Create a sweater, for example

Northbound

:26
:29
:33
:38
:42
:47
:52

Lightweight metal
Seaweed variety
Bean often "refried"
Kissers
Protagonist in bossy kids' game
Person of greater age

Rearrangement 9-10

Rearrange the letters in REAL RECENT TV to spell a type of accommodation you might have seen in a TV ad.

Rearrange the letters in ARTIST STUPOR to spell some attractions that must've been conceived in a fever dream.

Skyscrapers & Alleys 4

Place a skyscraper in each square, with a height from 1 to 6, so that no two buildings in the same row or column have the same number of floors. Each number outside of the grid represents the number of buildings visible when looking into the grid from the clue. Taller buildings block shorter buildings from view. Each number inside an alley represents the total number of buildings visible looking outward from its position.

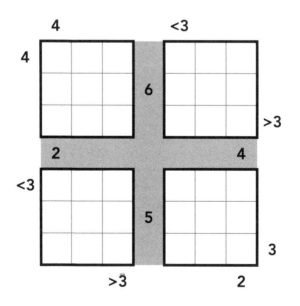

Rebus Travel Agency 4

This travel agency has some unusual ways of advertising travel destinations. Can you figure out where they want to send travelers?

Symbol Sums 4

The sums of five combinations of symbols have been provided. What is the value of each individual symbol?

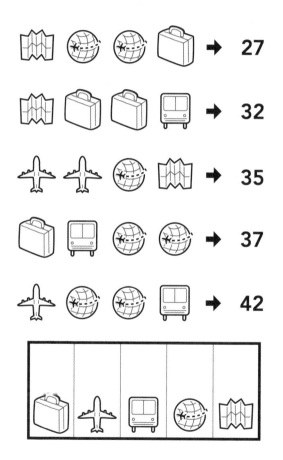

Numcross 6

Use the provided clues to fill the grid with numbers. No entry may start with a 0.

A	B	C		D	E	F
G				H		
I			J			
	K	L			M	
		N			O	P
Q	R			S		
T				U		

Across

A. N across × 9

D. E down + G across

G. F down × 4

H. Consecutive digits in ascending order

I. Q down − 2

J. E down − 7

K. Contains one of each even digit

N. Square root of G across

O. N across in reverse

Q. H across in reverse

S. A perfect square

T. Q across − 500

U. J across squared

Down

A. Digits that sum to J across

B. T across × 6

C. Highway number of "The Mother Road"

D. E down × P down

E. Sum of the digits in D down

F. Another perfect square

J. G across − I across

L. Digits that sum to S down

M. Two pairs of even digits

P. A palindrome

Q. F down in reverse

R. J across × 8

S. E down + 3

Scenic Route 4

Use the clues to determine pairs of words that fit the blanks provided.
Each pair will feature one shorter word with only some of the letters,
and one longer word that features all of the letters. When complete,
the numbered blanks will spell the name of a travel destination.

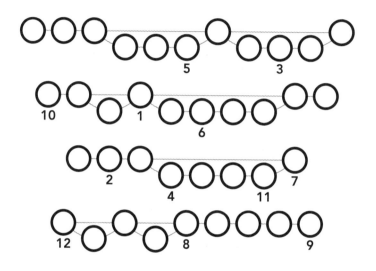

Faster Routes

Beautiful language

Cut into small cubes

Lower part of the face

Place to find a train

Scenic Routes

Circumstances

Incremental

Kids

Released

Country Road 4

Draw a single, continuous, nonintersecting loop moving through the grid and visiting each boldly-outlined region exactly once. A region displaying a number indicates the number of cells visited in that region. Non-visited cells from two different regions mustn't share an edge.

Throwing Shade 5

Shade some cells so the remaining letters in each row and column spell answers to the provided clues. Clues are sorted alphabetically by answer.

D	F	L	E	U	S	E	H	D
D	R	I	E	N	A	M	S	E
I	C	S	C	S	U	C	Y	E
C	A	E	R	G	G	E	A	L
I	B	A	C	O	G	N	E	D
R	A	P	H	L	L	E	E	S
I	L	C	H	Y	Y	M	N	N
R	S	N	O	W	Y	H	A	L
T	Y	P	P	C	O	O	L	D

Rows

- Flavored as whisky is
- Some ginger drinks
- Fantasy
- Item before or after chicken
- Clear with water
- Spiritual song
- Like some winter weather
- Queenly
- Mistake

Columns

- Garden medium
- Internet service option
- Repeat
- Come apart
- Laughing animal
- Every fourth year (mostly)
- Brief message
- Droopy
- Not aesthetic

Word Sudoku 3

Place one of each letter from LAKE HURON into each row, column, and 3 × 3 box without repetition.

L			U			A	K	
	A			N			U	R
		K			E			L
U			E					O
	E			H			A	
O					U			K
N			L			R		
E	K			A			O	
	R	U			O			N

Transit Map 5

Use the clues to fill the bus route with letters to form words both northbound and southbound.

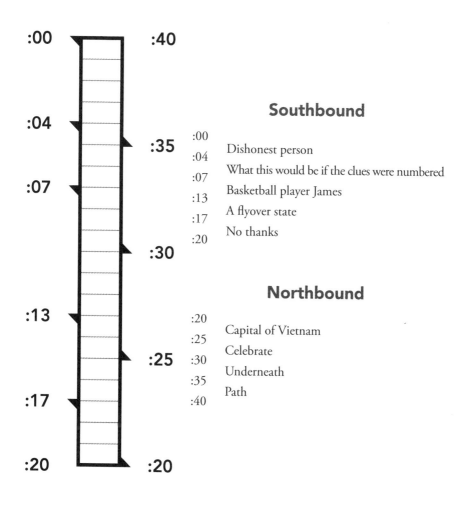

:00   **:40**

:04

:35

:07

:30

:13

:25

:17

:20   **:20**

Southbound

:00
:04   Dishonest person
:07   What this would be if the clues were numbered
:13   Basketball player James
:17   A flyover state
:20   No thanks

Northbound

:20
:25   Capital of Vietnam
:30   Celebrate
:35   Underneath
:40   Path

Skyscrapers & Alleys 5

Place a skyscraper in each square, with a height from 1 to 8, so that no two buildings in the same row or column have the same number of floors. Each number outside of the grid represents the number of buildings visible when looking into the grid from the clue. Taller buildings block shorter buildings from view. Each number inside an alley represents the total number of buildings visible looking outward from its position.

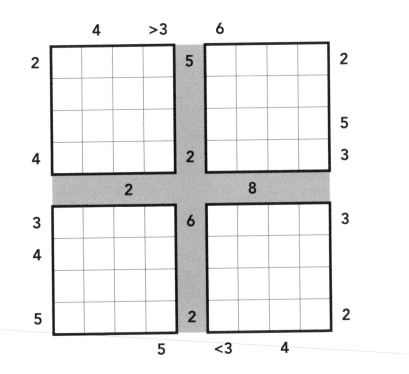

Cube Logic 6

Which of the four foldable patterns can be folded to make the crate displayed?

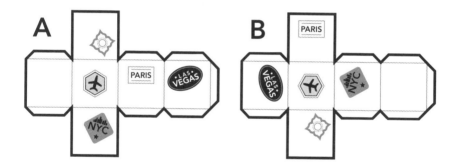

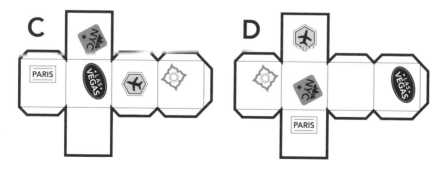

Rebus Travel Agency 5

This travel agency has some unusual ways of advertising travel destinations. Can you figure out where they want to send travelers?

Rearrangement 11-12

Rearrange the letters in FILE ANNOTATORS to spell a place that some park rangers might document a bigfoot sighting.

Rearrange the letters in AVERT TANGLE to spell someone who will smooth out all the details of your vacation for you.

Numcross 7

Use the provided clues to fill the grid with numbers. No entry may start with a 0.

A	B		C	D	E		F	G
H			I				J	
K		L			M	N		
O				P				
		Q	R			S	T	U
V	W		X		Y		Z	
AA		BB		CC		DD		
		EE	FF			GG	HH	II
JJ	KK				LL			
MM			NN	OO			PP	
QQ			RR				SS	

Across

A. Sum of the even digits in A down

C. A palindrome

F. A multiple of Z across

H. Sum of the digits along the longest diagonal of unshaded squares in the puzzle

I. S across − 7

J. D down in reverse

K. E down + J across

M. The digits of E down in descending order

O. AA across + RR across

P. A multiple of SS across

Q. C down × 8

S. JJ down in reverse

V. D down + 1

X. Another palindrome

Z. Sum of the digits in D down

AA. R down + 10

CC. Z across × PP across

EE. OO down × QQ across

GG. PP across × 7

JJ. L down × 9

LL. X across × 3

MM. SS across in reverse

NN. AA across × 7

PP. OO down + 1

QQ. A perfect square

RR. X across − GG across

SS. A perfect cube

Down

A. An even number whose digits sum to 13

B. F across × OO down

C. D down × 2

D. F across + 1

E. Year that President Clinton's second term began

F. Consecutive digits in ascending order

G. RR across + V down

L. Consecutive digits in ascending order

N. Q across + 5

P. Contains one of every even digit

R. F across + H across

T. U down + 10

U. QQ across in reverse

V. OO down + Z across

W. Y down − 5

Y. V across in reverse

BB. NN across + Z across

DD. PP across × the digit that isn't represented in the longest diagonal of unshaded cells in the puzzle

FF. V across × Y down

HH. Consists of even digits in descending order

II. Another palindrome

JJ. U down × Z across

KK. H across × 3

LL. GG across + 3

OO. P down ÷ JJ down

Throwing Shade 6

Shade some cells so the remaining letters in each row and column spell answers to the provided clues. Clues are sorted alphabetically by answer.

T	H	H	E	S	E	M	E	D
H	A	E	L	E	D	E	L	S
R	R	A	D	B	B	I	T	O
E	V	E	E	V	S	M	E	N
T	H	R	A	A	T	I	L	E
F	F	A	E	E	E	N	C	E
O	L	O	C	N	O	T	E	T
E	A	A	T	S	M	Y	C	Y
G	G	R	R	E	E	T	T	E

Rows

- Lacking difficulty
- Equal
- Divisive structure
- Say "Hi"
- The bad place
- Chunk of land
- Car feature
- Big rodent
- Topical

Columns

- Over with
- Senior
- Vote into office
- Fabric creation
- Notice a sound
- Common toothpaste flavor
- Small number
- Lower digit
- Flower holder

Rows Garden 5

Using the clues provided, enter a letter into each triangle to fill the garden. Each row contains one or two entries, and each hexagonal flower contains a six-letter word wrapped around the center. It's up to you to determine where to place the starting letter and the direction of the word.

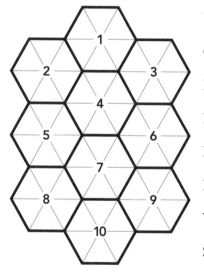

Uncooked

Coastal bird / Remove

Biblical brother / White-barked tree

Blender setting / Gal with attitude

Place for vehicles / Game day chicken dish

Preserved like some spices / Hit hard and accurately

When pigs fly / Rapport, inf.

Sticky material

Flowers

1. Bros. known for film studio
2. Coupon for a partial refund
3. Golden fast-food logo feature
4. Suitable for consumption
5. Furor
6. Keeping for later
7. Out of breath
8. Highly motivated
9. Get off track
10. Impact site

Country Road 5

Draw a single, continuous, nonintersecting loop moving through the grid and visiting each boldly-outlined region exactly once. A region displaying a number indicates the number of cells visited in that region. Non-visited cells from two different regions mustn't share an edge.

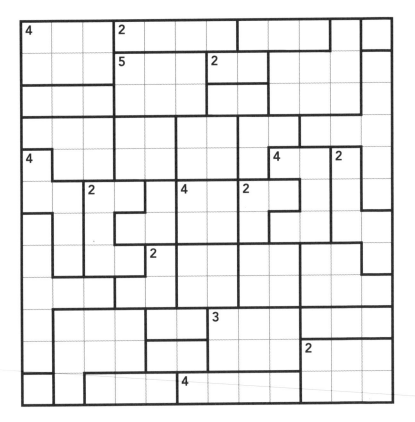

Word Sudoku 4

Place one of each letter from PHOENIX, AZ into each row, column, and 3 × 3 box without repetition.

	Z	N		H				
I	P		X					Z
		I				X	A	
	A	X			I			
O				N				H
		E				Z	X	
	H	O			E			
P					Z		N	I
			X			A	O	

Rows Garden 6

Using the clues provided, enter a letter into each triangle to fill the garden. Each row contains one or two entries, and each hexagonal flower contains a six-letter word wrapped around the center. It's up to you to determine where to place the starting letter and the direction of the word.

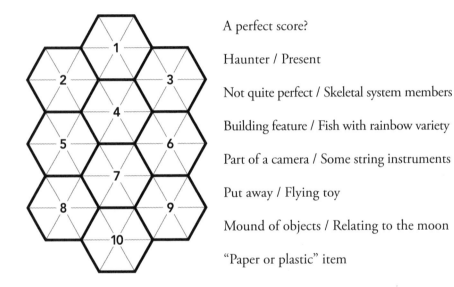

A perfect score?

Haunter / Present

Not quite perfect / Skeletal system members

Building feature / Fish with rainbow variety

Part of a camera / Some string instruments

Put away / Flying toy

Mound of objects / Relating to the moon

"Paper or plastic" item

Flowers

1.   Celiac sufferer's woe

2.   Diligently practicing

3.   Most intricate

4.   Actor Downey Jr.

5.   Ramen component

6.   Baby plant

7.   Bartender necessity

8.   Some airline staff

9.   Eye component

10. Type of whale

Rebus Travel Agency 6

This travel agency has some unusual ways of advertising travel destinations. Can you figure out where they want to send travelers?

BEACH

Scenic Route 5

Use the clues to determine pairs of words that fit the blanks provided. Each pair will feature one shorter word with only some of the letters, and one longer word that features all of the letters. When complete, the numbered blanks will spell the name of a travel destination.

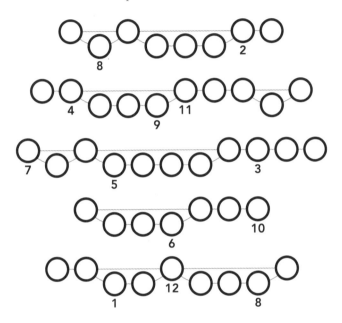

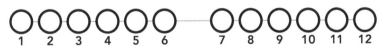

Faster Routes

Arduous journey

Bring together

Feel sorry for one

Persuade with a reward

Substance used in jellies

Scenic Routes

Degree of accuracy

Elderly matriarch

More important

Legal registration of a name

Relaxation time

Symbol Sums 5

The sums of five combinations of symbols have been provided. What is the value of each individual symbol?

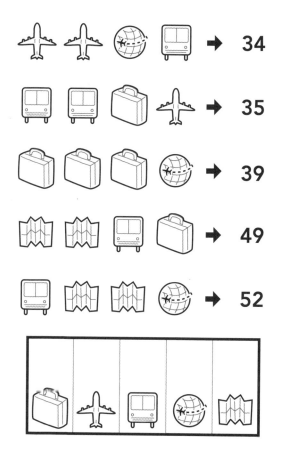

Cube Logic 7

Which of the four foldable patterns can be folded to make the crate displayed?

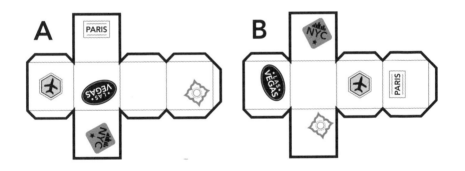

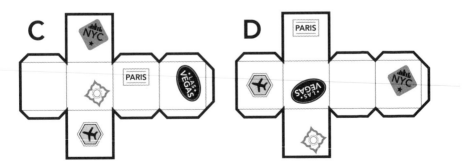

Rearrangement 13-14

Rearrange the letters in TARMAC RELIANCE to spell a part of the world with many destinations to which you can fly.

Rearrange the letters in CRITICAL TECH REC. to spell a part of the world where adequate heating is a vital part of life.

Numcross 8

Use the provided clues to fill the grid with numbers. No entry may start with a 0.

Across

A.	C down in reverse
C.	A across × 4
F.	A perfect cube
H.	F across − 4
I.	B down × 3
J.	Digits that sum to PP across
K.	J across × 7
M.	Digits that sum to C down
O.	Digits that sum to H across
R.	E down × 3
T.	GG down + 2
W.	A perfect square
X.	A palindrome
Z.	Sum of the digits in Q down
AA.	BB down in reverse
CC.	Q down × 4
EE.	A "full house"
GG.	KK down × 3
II.	PP across × SS across
LL.	NN down − 5
MM.	L down − 4
PP.	SS across − 6
QQ.	OO down + 4
RR.	OO down × 3
SS.	PP across + 6

Down

A.	A multiple of Z across
B.	R down − F across
C.	A across in reverse
D.	A across + 20
E.	One-third of R across
F.	A across × 7
G.	C down + KK down
L.	MM across + 4
N.	T across + PP across
P.	D down × 7
Q.	Contains one of each odd digit
R.	A multiple of PP across
S.	L down × 2
U.	OO down × 8
V.	Z across × 6
Y.	Q down ÷ Z across
BB.	L down × 5
DD.	II across × 3
FF.	AA across × 9
GG.	Digits that sum to SS across
HH.	LL across × 2
JJ.	KK down + QQ across
KK.	Another palindrome
NN.	X across ÷ PP across
OO.	NN down + H across

Throwing Shade 7

Shade some cells so the remaining letters in each row and column spell answers to the provided clues. Clues are sorted alphabetically by answer.

N	F	I	O	E	C	D	G	E
L	M	H	U	A	L	S	T	S
A	I	I	S	M	L	K	E	N
T	S	D	T	U	O	R	R	M
T	S	R	C	A	A	I	L	M
U	T	R	A	M	B	H	O	U
R	I	O	C	W	K	Y	A	H
E	S	N	R	V	Y	E	R	Y
K	T	E	K	E	N	R	N	Y

Rows

- Space on a plane
- A deadly sin
- Barbie's partner
- Ship component
- Extended family member
- Iconic Stallone character
- Weather varietal
- Type of transit vehicle
- State home to Zion National Park

Columns

- Conceal
- Roof part
- Big entertainment award
- Laundry gadget
- Lightly spray
- Demeanor
- Timid
- Make a tower
- Type of bird

Transit Map 6

Use the clues to fill the bus route with letters to form words both northbound and southbound.

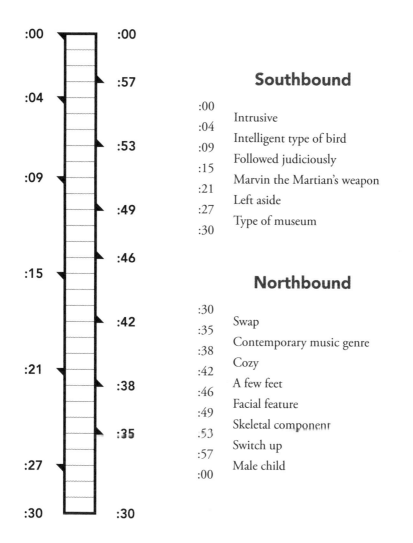

Southbound

:00	
:04	Intrusive
:09	Intelligent type of bird
:15	Followed judiciously
:21	Marvin the Martian's weapon
:27	Left aside
:30	Type of museum

Northbound

:30	
:35	Swap
:38	Contemporary music genre
:42	Cozy
:46	A few feet
:49	Facial feature
:53	Skeletal component
:57	Switch up
:00	Male child

Cube Logic 8

Which of the four foldable patterns can be folded to make the crate displayed?

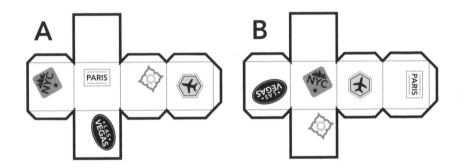

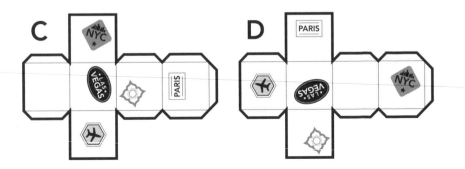

Skyscrapers & Alleys 6

Place a skyscraper in each square, with a height from 1 to 8, so that no two buildings in the same row or column have the same number of floors. Each number outside of the grid represents the number of buildings visible when looking into the grid from the clue. Taller buildings block shorter buildings from view. Each number inside an alley represents the total number of buildings visible looking outward from its position.

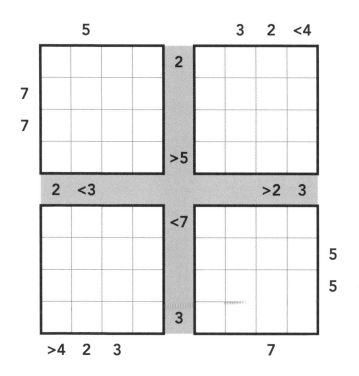

Symbol Sums 6

The sums of five combinations of symbols have been provided. What is the value of each individual symbol?

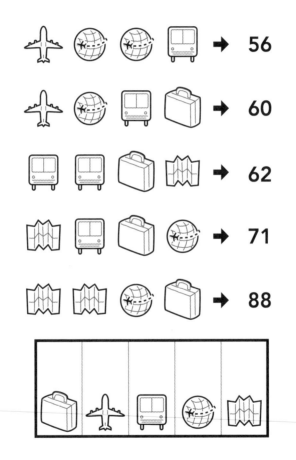

Rows Garden 7

Using the clues provided, enter a letter into each triangle to fill the garden. Each row contains one or two entries, and each hexagonal flower contains a six-letter word wrapped around the center. It's up to you to determine where to place the starting letter and the direction of the word.

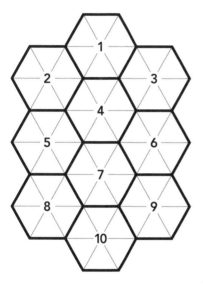

Nada

Hopping amphibian / Boxing match

The floor, to kids? / Wet and sticky

Fad / Unit of land size

Trainee / Table-like rock structure

Sport equipment / A certain pair of organs

Frozen protagonist / Torso wear

Potential pronoun

Flowers

1.	Cabinet type	**6.**	Fold
2.	Variety of food or beverage	**7.**	Hairstyle making a comeback
3.	Capable and powerful	**8.**	Like some stickers on mail
4.	Mortal enemy of a sock	**9.**	Yo-yo part
5.	Withhold	**10.**	Go over again

Rearrangement 15-16

Rearrange the letters in OTHERS' SUITES to spell the folks hanging out where you live while you're on vacation.

Rearrange the letters in DECOR SNAPSHOT to spell a general location where you might need to rely on photos before booking lodging.

Country Road 6

Draw a single, continuous, nonintersecting loop moving through the grid and visiting each boldly-outlined region exactly once. A region displaying a number indicates the number of cells visited in that region. Non-visited cells from two different regions mustn't share an edge.

Throwing Shade 8

Shade some cells so the remaining letters in each row and column spell answers to the provided clues. Clues are sorted alphabetically by answer.

V	I	D	C	W	F	E	O	R
A	R	R	C	W	B	H	I	G
O	H	R	E	A	L	E	L	E
T	O	U	P	S	I	E	E	R
T	R	U	N	I	C	C	I	E
T	A	N	O	R	K	A	L	E
E	T	O	C	H	V	O	E	D
R	F	K	I	K	I	N	D	Y
R	E	A	A	H	D	D	Y	Y

Rows

- Part of the foot
- Cut into
- Considerate and pleasant
- Verbal or mouth-related
- Prepared
- Formal address
- Agreement
- Something watched
- Hairpiece

Columns

- One of the "three-letter agencies"
- Inebriated
- Bring to a conclusion
- Full of avarice
- Fuming
- Beat easily
- Lubricated
- Entity in an election
- Clean

Rows Garden 8

Using the clues provided, enter a letter into each triangle to fill the garden. Each row contains one or two entries, and each hexagonal flower contains a six-letter word wrapped around the center. It's up to you to determine where to place the starting letter and the direction of the word.

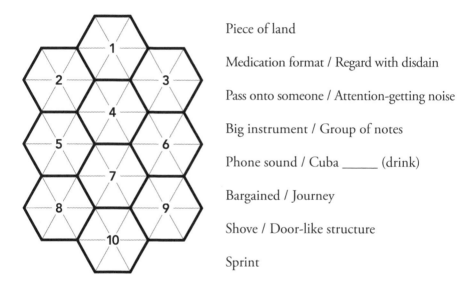

Piece of land

Medication format / Regard with disdain

Pass onto someone / Attention-getting noise

Big instrument / Group of notes

Phone sound / Cuba _____ (drink)

Bargained / Journey

Shove / Door-like structure

Sprint

Flowers

1.	Voting utility	6.	Boundary
2.	Loot	7.	Small
3.	Summer garb	8.	Zombie-like
4.	Spread the word	9.	Seafaring thief
5.	Shirt fastener	10.	Rock/metal offshoot

Rebus Travel Agency 7

This travel agency has some unusual ways of advertising travel destinations. Can you figure out where they want to send travelers?

EEEEEEE

Symbol Sums 7

The sums of five combinations of symbols have been provided. What is the value of each individual symbol?

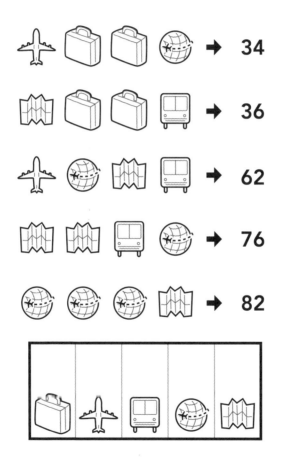

Transit Map 7

Use the clues to fill the bus route with letters to form words both northbound and southbound.

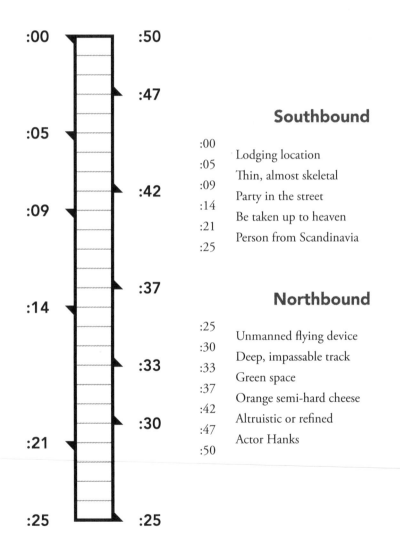

Southbound

:00
:05   Lodging location
:09   Thin, almost skeletal
:14   Party in the street
:21   Be taken up to heaven
:25   Person from Scandinavia

Northbound

:25
:30   Unmanned flying device
:33   Deep, impassable track
:37   Green space
:42   Orange semi-hard cheese
:47   Altruistic or refined
:50   Actor Hanks

Rebus Travel Agency 8

This travel agency has some unusual ways of advertising travel destinations. Can you figure out where they want to send travelers?

SU 🖊 LA

🖊

Numcross 9

Use the provided clues to fill the grid with numbers. No entry may start with a 0.

A	B	C		D	E		F	G
H				I			J	
		K	L		M	N		
	O			P		Q		
R				S	T			
U			V				W	X
		Y					Z	
	AA			BB	CC	DD		
EE			FF		GG			
HH			II	JJ		KK	LL	MM
NN			OO			PP		

Across

A.	One-third O across
D.	D down + 2
F.	MM down – 6
H.	HH across + W down
I.	R across + 1
J.	II across × 5
K.	A perfect square
M.	Consecutive digits not in order
O.	Year the Hollywood sign (originally "Hollywoodland") was created
Q.	W across × 2
R.	One-third OO across
S.	X down × 2
U.	Sum of the digits in AA down
V.	EE across ÷ 3
W.	II across + 1
Y.	D across × F across
Z.	F across × 3
AA.	K across × 3
BB.	DD down in reverse
EE.	C down + 4
GG.	F across + 1
HH.	D down × 3
II.	Another perfect square
KK.	FF down + PP across
NN.	MM down + 1
OO.	MM down × 2
PP.	J across + MM down

Down

A.	Z across – 2
B.	Another perfect square
C.	One-fifth M across
D.	Sum of the digits in A across
E.	KK across – K across
F.	BB across × 2
G.	F across × 5
L.	D across × 4
N.	A palindrome
O.	A down × 3
P.	A "full house"
R.	F across in reverse
T.	F across + LL down
V.	X down – II across
W.	OO across × 3
X.	JJ down + 9
Y.	U across × D down
AA.	M across – PP across
CC.	F across × 2
DD.	BB across in reverse
EE.	D down × R down
FF.	G down × 3
JJ.	A perfect cube
LL.	One-fourth I across
MM.	Another perfect cube

Throwing Shade 9

Shade some cells so the remaining letters in each row and column spell answers to the provided clues. Clues are sorted alphabetically by answer.

A	G	R	E	O	S	E	G	S
N	A	J	A	S	R	A	A	S
C	U	O	R	L	I	N	G	P
R	A	J	S	A	R	R	E	S
B	A	N	A	S	N	L	A	P
H	O	O	L	C	K	E	L	Y
O	R	C	I	H	I	D	N	D
L	D	Y	E	H	Y	Y	E	Y
O	S	K	Y	T	A	I	T	N

Rows

- Like forever
- Urgent Deadline
- Icy sport
- Recolor
- Boughs used in Christmas decor
- Some containers
- Rocket propulsion group
- Type of flower
- The atmosphere and beyond

Columns

- Type of pepper
- *Toy Story* character
- Ahead of schedule
- Mighty wind
- Security forces
- Sporty person
- Iconic digital assistant
- Tear through
- Covert operative

Cube Logic 9

Which of the four foldable patterns can be folded to make the crate displayed?

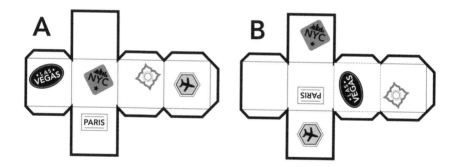

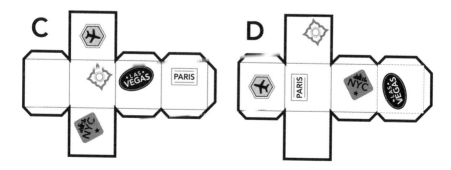

Transit Map 8

Use the clues to fill the bus route with letters to form words both northbound and southbound.

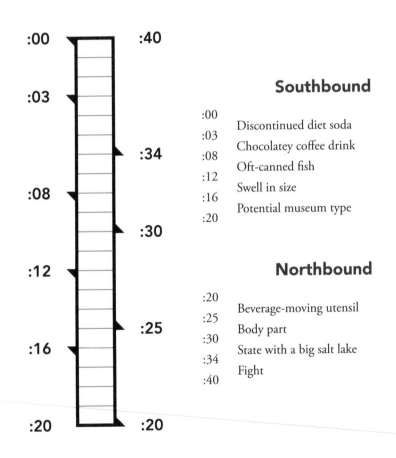

Southbound

:00
:03 — Discontinued diet soda
:08 — Chocolatey coffee drink
:12 — Oft-canned fish
:16 — Swell in size
:20 — Potential museum type

Northbound

:20
:25 — Beverage-moving utensil
:30 — Body part
:34 — State with a big salt lake
:40 — Fight

Symbol Sums 8

The sums of five combinations of symbols have been provided. What is the value of each individual symbol?

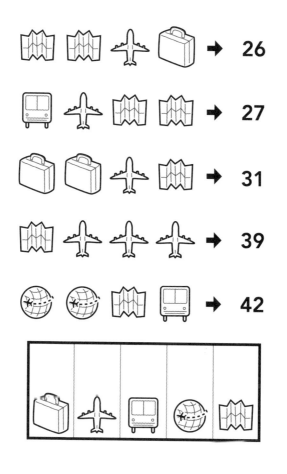

Numcross 10

Use the provided clues to fill the grid with numbers. No entry may start with a 0.

A	B		C	D	E		F	G
H			I				J	
K		L			M	N		
O				P				
		Q	R			S	T	U
V	W		X		Y		Z	
AA		BB		CC		DD		
		EE	FF			GG	HH	II
JJ	KK				LL			
MM			NN	OO			PP	
QQ			RR				SS	

Across

A. V across + OO down
C. Consecutive digits not in order
F. J across in reverse
H. A perfect square
I. G down × 3
J. A perfect cube
K. Consecutive digits not in order
M. Number of feet in one mile
O. C across + OO down
P. Z across × D down
Q. One-fifth of K across
S. One-fifth of HH down
V. C down ÷ V down
X. G down + the sum of the digits in X across
Z. A multiple of J across
AA. Consecutive digits not in order
CC. H across × V across
EE. A multiple of D down
GG. A number between C across and G down
JJ. Digits that sum to V down
LL. The digits of A across and V across in some order
MM. One-third of C across
NN. A multiple of K down
PP. SS across − D down
QQ. PP across × 2
RR. Digits that sum to V across
SS. J across × 2

Down

A. Two pair
B. One-fourth of JJ across
C. C across + F across
D. A factor of EE across
E. Digits that sum to Y down
F. U down × 8
G. A multiple of J across
L. A multiple of GG across
N. F across × 3
P. A "full house"
R. OO down × 2
T. J across + 1
U. F across + V down
V. C down ÷ V across
W. A multiple of V down
Y. The odd digits that aren't in row 5 of the grid
BB. Digits that sum to OO down
DD. A palindrome
FF. S across × 2
HH. E down + QQ across
II. A multiple of LL down
JJ. Consecutive digits in ascending order
KK. A multiple of F across
LL. V across + QQ across
OO. J across − 1

Answer Keys

Country Road 1

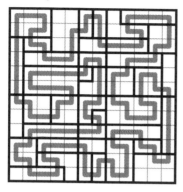

Country Road 2

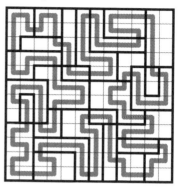

Country Road 3

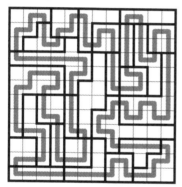

Country Road 4

Country Road 5

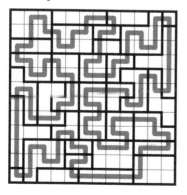

Country Road 6

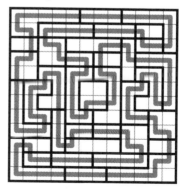

Cube Logic

1. D and F
2. A and B
3. D and E
4. C
5. A
6. B
7. B
8. C
9. B

Numcross 1

1	2	1	■	1	3	2
3	0	0	■	6	1	0
4	9	■	■	1	6	■
■	1	9	3	7	5	■
■	■	2	5	■	1	1
6	2	0	■	1	1	0
7	7	5	■	2	5	0

Numcross 2

2	5	2	■	■	1	1
5	3	5	9	■	1	7
1	3	■	7	2	7	5
■	■	2	3	1	■	■
1	1	2	5	■	8	7
2	7	■	1	9	2	5
6	4	■	■	1	7	6

Numcross 3

2	7	■	■	1	3	■
4	9	■	4	6	2	■
8	8	8	5	5	■	■
1	6	2	■	2	4	2
■	6	6	8	1	0	■
■	1	4	4	■	3	0
■	5	0	■	■	2	1

Numcross 4

2	5	■	■	■	7	4
6	8	2	8	■	7	9
■	■	1	9	6	6	■
■	1	2	■	2	4	■
■	6	3	6	9	■	■
6	0	■	1	9	4	1
4	0	■	■	■	7	5

Numcross 5

6	3	1	■	■	2	2
4	4	7	7	■	2	7
■	1	3	7	9	5	■
2	2	4	■	4	9	9
8	8	2	8	2	■	■
2	5	■	9	1	1	9
3	7	■	■	1	0	8

Numcross 6

1	2	6	■	2	1	4
1	9	6	■	7	8	9
9	2	■	1	1	■	■
■	2	6	0	8	4	■
■	1	4	■	4	1	■
9	8	7	■	2	2	5
4	8	7	■	1	2	1

Numcross 7

Numcross 8

Numcross 9

Numcross 10

Rearrangement

1. Santa Monica Pier
2. First Class Lounge
3. Bottle of Sunscreen
4. Bed and Breakfast
5. Brief Layover
6. Cruise Director
7. Souvenir Stands
8. Gondola Rental
9. Travel Center
10. Tourist Traps
11. National Forest
12. Travel Agent
13. Central America
14. The Arctic Circle
15. House Sitters
16. Across the Pond

Rebus Travel Agency

1. Toronto
2. Indiana
3. Tokyo
4. Thunder Bay, Ontario
5. Round Rock, Texas
6. White Sand Beach
7. Belize
8. Upper Peninsula

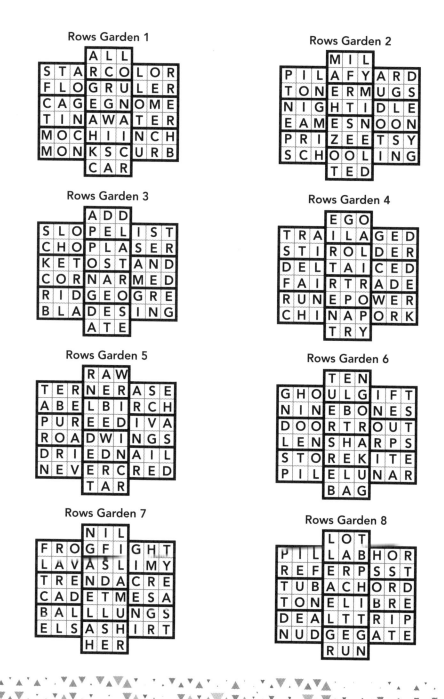

Rows Garden 1

```
      A L L
S T A R C O L O R
F L O G R U L E R
C A G E G N O M E
T I N A W A T E R
M O C H I I N C H
M O N K S C U R B
      C A R
```

Rows Garden 2

```
      M I L
P I L A F Y A R D
T O N E R M U G S
N I G H T I D L E
E A M E S N O O N
P R I Z E E T S Y
S C H O O L I N G
      T E D
```

Rows Garden 3

```
      A D D
S L O P E L I S T
C H O P L A S E R
K E T O S T A N D
C O R N A R M E D
R I D G E O G R E
B L A D E S I N G
      A T E
```

Rows Garden 4

```
      E G O
T R A I L A G E D
S T I R O L D E R
D E L T A I C E D
F A I R T R A D E
R U N E P O W E R
C H I N A P O R K
      T R Y
```

Rows Garden 5

```
      R A W
T E R N E R A S E
A B E L B I R C H
P U R E E D I V A
R O A D W I N G S
D R I E D N A I L
N E V E R C R E D
      T A R
```

Rows Garden 6

```
      T E N
G H O U L G I F T
N I N E B O N E S
D O O R T R O U T
L E N S H A R P S
S T O R E K I T E
P I L E L U N A R
      B A G
```

Rows Garden 7

```
      N I L
F R O G F I G H T
L A V A S L I M Y
T R E N D A C R E
C A D E T M E S A
B A L L L U N G S
E L S A S H I R T
      H E R
```

Rows Garden 8

```
      L O T
P I L L A B H O R
R E F E R P S S T
T U B A C H O R D
T O N E L I B R E
D E A L T T R I P
N U D G E G A T E
      R U N
```

Scenic Route 1

Intentional / International
Pecan / Pelican
Refer / Refresher
Paris, France

Scenic Route 2

Scorn / Scorpion
Stale / Streamline
Diary / Dictionary
Pork / Patchwork
Wichita, Kansas

Scenic Route 3

Bury / Buttery
Dicey / Discovery
Frog / Frowning
Term / Thunderstorm
Secular / Spectacular
San Luis Obispo

Scenic Route 4

Prose / Progressive
Diced / Discharged
Chin / Children
Station / Situation
Chilean Andes

Scenic Route 5

Pity / Priority
Pectin / Perfection
Gather / Grandmother
Lure / Leisure
Trek / Trademark
Athens, Greece

Skyscrapers & Alleys 1

2	4	6		1	3	5
1	2	3		5	4	6
4	3	1		6	5	2

5	1	2		4	6	3
6	5	4		3	2	1
3	6	5		2	1	4

Skyscrapers & Alleys 2

4	3	1		6	5	2
6	5	4		2	3	1
1	2	3		5	6	4

3	6	2		1	4	5
5	1	6		4	2	3
2	4	5		3	1	6

Skyscrapers & Alleys 3

2	4	1		6	3	5
6	5	4		1	2	3
1	6	3		5	4	2

3	2	5		4	6	1
4	1	2		3	5	6
5	3	6		2	1	4

Skyscrapers & Alleys 4

2	3	4		6	1	5
3	2	1		4	5	6
4	5	6		3	2	1

6	1	5		2	4	3
5	4	3		1	6	2
1	6	2		5	3	4

Skyscrapers & Alleys 5

7	3	5	1		2	8	4	6
6	5	4	2		3	7	8	1
8	7	6	3		4	5	1	2
3	4	7	8		6	1	2	5

5	6	8	7		1	2	3	4
4	1	2	6		5	3	7	8
2	8	1	5		7	4	6	3
1	2	3	4		8	6	5	7

Skyscrapers & Alleys 6

3	1	5	6		8	2	4	7
1	2	3	4		5	7	8	6
2	3	4	5		1	6	7	8
8	7	1	2		4	5	6	3

7	8	6	3		2	1	5	4
6	5	8	1		7	4	3	2
5	4	7	8		6	3	2	1
4	6	2	7		3	8	1	5

Story Logic 1

- A. Taco Lo Quiero served Green Chile Corn and raffled at 5:00 PM.
- B. Crepe Fusion served Seasoned Fries and raffled at 4:15 PM.
- C. Terry's BBQ served Tex-Mex Corn and raffled at 7:15 PM.
- D. Quill and Quark served Truffle Mac and raffled at 6:30 PM.
- E. Smokin' Hawg Q served Bacon Green Beans and raffled at 3:30 PM.
- F. Taqueria Ana Luisa served Potato Salad and raffled at 5:45 PM.

Story Logic 2

- 10:15 AM Jorge departs for Tulsa.
- 11:45 AM Glen departs for San Diego.
- 1:30 PM Ike departs for Reno.
- 3:00 PM Hilda departs for Pasadena.

Story Logic 3

- Becky was assigned to wear the horse costume near the exit.
- Celia was assigned to wear the frog costume near the drop tower.
- Dennis was assigned to wear the iguana costume near the bumper cars.
- Enrique was assigned to wear the gopher costume near the chip shop.

Symbol Sums 1

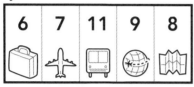

9	19	17	12	10

Symbol Sums 2

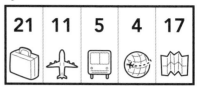

21	11	5	4	17

Symbol Sums 3

6	7	11	9	8

Symbol Sums 4

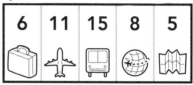

6	11	15	8	5

Symbol Sums 5

9	6	10	12	15

Symbol Sums 6

21	14	8	17	25

Symbol Sums 7

2	11	7	19	25

Symbol Sums 8

8	12	9	15	3

Throwing Shade 1

Throwing Shade 2

Throwing Shade 3

Throwing Shade 4

Throwing Shade 5

Throwing Shade 6

Throwing Shade 7

Throwing Shade 8

Throwing Shade 9

Transit Map 1

Southbound
:00
:05 Debit
:11 Ornate
:16 Caper
:22 Admire
:25 Nod

Northbound
:25
:29 Done
:32 Rim
:36 Dare
:40 Pace
:43 Tan
:47 Roti
:50 Bed

Transit Map 2

Southbound
:00
:04 Yarn
:07 Ago
:11 Help
:17 Rupees
:20 Nub
:23 Mob

Northbound
:23
:27 Bomb
:32 Unsee
:38 Purple
:43 Hogan
:46 Ray

Transit Map 3

Southbound
:00
:04 Mach
:08 Sale
:12 Yeti
:17 Abort
:25 Embalmed

Northbound
:25
:28 Dem
:31 Lab
:36 Metro
:40 Bait
:47 Eyelash
:50 Cam

Transit Map 4

Southbound
:00
:03 Red
:07 Leno
:11 Miss
:16 Pilot
:22 Nipple
:26 Knit

Northbound
:26
:29 Tin
:33 Kelp
:38 Pinto
:42 Lips
:47 Simon
:52 Elder

Transit Map 5

Southbound

:00	
:04	Liar
:07	Two
:13	Lebron
:17	Ohio
:20	Nah

Northbound

:20	
:25	Hanoi
:30	Honor
:35	Below
:40	Trail

Transit Map 6

Southbound

:00	
:04	Nosy
:09	Raven
:15	Obeyed
:21	Raygun
:27	Spared
:30	Art

Northbound

:30	
:35	Trade
:38	Rap
:42	Snug
:46	Yard
:49	Eye
:53	Bone
:57	Vary
:00	Son

Transit Map 7

Southbound

:00	
:05	Motel
:09	Bony
:14	Block
:21	Rapture
:25	Nord

Northbound

:25	
:30	Drone
:33	Rut
:37	Park
:42	Colby
:47	Noble
:50	Tom

Transit Map 8

Southbound

:00	
:03	Tab
:08	Mocha
:12	Tuna
:16	Grow
:20	Arts

Northbound

:20	
:25	Straw
:30	Organ
:34	Utah
:40	Combat

Word Sudoku 1

M	E	R	A	T	O	B	I	L
B	L	O	I	M	R	E	T	A
I	A	T	B	E	L	R	M	O
R	O	L	T	B	E	I	A	M
E	T	M	O	I	A	L	B	R
A	I	B	L	R	M	O	E	T
L	M	A	E	O	I	T	R	B
T	R	I	M	L	B	A	O	E
O	B	E	R	A	T	M	L	I

Word Sudoku 2

N	D	R	E	A	O	S	I	P
I	P	A	S	R	N	O	D	E
E	S	O	I	D	P	N	A	R
S	A	N	D	O	R	P	E	I
R	O	D	P	I	E	A	N	S
P	I	E	N	S	A	D	R	O
O	N	P	A	E	I	R	S	D
A	E	S	R	P	D	I	O	N
D	R	I	O	N	S	E	P	A

Word Sudoku 3

L	O	N	U	R	H	A	K	E
H	A	E	K	N	L	O	U	R
R	U	K	A	O	E	H	N	L
U	L	H	E	K	A	N	R	O
K	E	R	O	H	N	L	A	U
O	N	A	R	L	U	E	H	K
N	H	O	L	U	K	R	E	A
E	K	L	N	A	R	U	O	H
A	R	U	H	E	O	K	L	N

Word Sudoku 4

X	Z	N	P	H	A	E	I	O
I	P	A	X	E	O	N	H	Z
E	O	H	I	Z	N	X	A	P
H	A	X	Z	P	I	O	E	N
O	E	Z	A	N	X	I	P	H
N	I	P	E	O	H	Z	X	A
A	H	O	N	I	E	P	Z	X
P	X	E	O	A	Z	H	N	I
Z	N	I	H	X	P	A	O	E

Exercise Your Mind at American Mensa

At American Mensa, we love puzzles. In fact, we have events—large and small—centered around games and puzzles.

Of course, with tens of thousands of members from ages 2 to 102, we are much more than that. Our one shared trait might be one you share, too: high intelligence, measured in the top 2 percent of the general public in a standardized test.

Get-togethers with other Mensans—from small pizza nights up to larger events like our annual Mind Games—are always stimulating and fun. Roughly 130 Special Interest Groups (we call them SIGs) offer the best of the real and virtual worlds. Highlighting the Mensa newsstand is our award-winning magazine, *Mensa Bulletin*, which stimulates the curious mind with unique features that add perspective to our fast-paced world.

And then there are the practical benefits of membership, such as exclusive offers through our partners and member discounts on magazine subscriptions, online shopping, and financial services.

Find out how to qualify or take our practice test at americanmensa.org/join.